Katrin Behrend

Guinea Pigs

Proper Care and Understanding

**Expert Advice
for Appropriate Maintenance**

Color photographs: Karin Skogstad

Illustrations: György Jankovics

Consulting Editor: Lucia Vriends-Parent

D0916417

BARRON'S

Contents

Foreword

How cute and appealing a little guinea pig can look, and if in addition it is a rough-coated one with the amusing whorls that occur in the most impossible places on the body, you simply lose your heart to such an animal. It's an ideal playmate for children, especially, because it's sociable, loves to be petted and cuddled, and will become even livelier the more attention it has and the better it is maintained in conformity with its needs and behavior patterns.

What is required for proper maintenance is explained by Katrin Behrend in this new Barron's Pet Owners Manual. She tells what to look for when buying a cage and equipment, what to watch out for in exercising so that nothing happens to the guinea pig—even how you might housebreak it, how to feed it properly, and what to do if it ever gets sick. All the instructions can be carried out easily, so that even a child can learn how to care for the animal.

Charming color photographs by Karin Skogstad, taken especially for this book, and many informative drawings by György Jankovics provide a living picture of this popular pet.

The author and editors wish you much pleasure with your guinea pig.

Guinea pigs are lively, entertaining animals that can give their keepers a great deal of pleasure. They need correct, loving care and stimulating occupation so that their instincts and their senses will be constantly challenged and they don't vegetate apathetically in their cage.

Please see the "Important Note" on page 63.

Things to Think About When Buying Guinea Pigs

When the guinea pig must be alone a great deal, it pines, for it is a social animal that in the wild lives in a herd. Anyone who is likely to be away from home all day long should get two guinea pigs. Two females get on especially well together.

The first pets I ever had as a child were a pair of guinea pigs. I saw these dear little creatures at a neighbor's and was enchanted. When she laid two of them in my lap, I felt I'd received a splendid present. Since she also gave me an old rabbit hutch in addition and promised always to provide me with enough hay, all problems appeared to have been solved. I was allowed to put the hutch on our gigantic balcony and went out every morning to get fresh green feed for my two little charges. Sometimes I took them to the meadow, too, but that often ended in a wild chase after them, since they crept into the most unreachable corners possible. When one morning I opened the hutch door and found four little guinea pigs instead of two, I was overjoyed. Of course, this "wonderful" reproduction began to repeat itself with the speed of the wind. Before very long, I had twelve guinea pigs falling all over themselves in the hutch, which by this time had grown much too small, and my mother put her foot down. At that time I knew next to nothing at all about these animals and their life-style. For even if they are easy to take care of, there are still some things you need to consider before you get any.

Ten Points to Consider

1. A guinea pig can live to be eight to ten years old. Are you prepared to be responsible for it for that long?

2. To enjoy life the guinea pig needs a large cage.

3. The cage must always be clean, the feed must always be fresh. Do you realize that this takes time and money?

4. A guinea pig is a social animal. It needs daily attention and exercise.

5. If you give a guinea pig to your child, you still need to keep an eye on the animal.

6. It's possible that the guinea pig will gnaw on carpets or furniture during exercise time or leave droppings or even vomit.

7. Remember that your guinea pig must also be looked after while you are away—such as for vacation or hospitalization.

8. Do you already have other pets who might not get along with a guinea pig?

9. If the guinea pig gets sick, you must take it to a veterinarian, which may turn out to be expensive.

10. Important: Find out before you buy a guinea pig whether you or any member of your family is allergic to animal fur.

Guinea pigs are ideal pets, especially for children. They become so tame that they love to take their treats right from the hand.

One or a Pair?

Since guinea pigs are social animals and in their natural habitat live together in a group, it's worth it to consider whether you want to get two animals at once.

A single animal is best for a child who wants it as a playmate. It will tame quickly and bond trustingly to the child as a partner. Of course you can't then relax the attention at some later point. If it's foreseeable that there's going to be too great a burden of homework or too much time will be devoted to a number of other interests, it's advisable to get a second animal that can be put with the first one as a companion later.

A pair is only advisable if you plan to breed them (page 41). As I mentioned at the beginning, guinea pigs are remarkably fast-breeding. You can reckon on offspring four to five times a year. It is, of course, wonderful to experience a guinea pig nursery of this sort, but "What shall we do with the babies?" gets to be a question that comes up too often.

Two females get along very well together in any case.

Two males begin to fight when they are grown, and they can inflict some bad bites. Therefore, you must have both animals castrated. This must be done by a veterinarian.

My advice: Let the female of a pair have some babies and then have the male castrated.

Male or Female?

Maintenance is also an important consideration in whether you opt to get a male or a female guinea pig.

A male, with the arrival of sexual maturity, gives off a strong scent, which disappears if you have the animal castrated at the age of nine to twelve months. Male guinea pigs grow larger and are also livelier.

A female is better for keeping in an apartment. She remains smaller, doesn't smell as strong as the male when she reaches sexual maturity, and is usually more affectionate. Of course, it can happen that the animal you bought was already pregnant at the time of sale or that your child takes her to play at the house of a friend who has a male. Without anyone's noticing, the female is bred and you have to deal with unwanted young.

Sex determination of young animals is difficult. Leave that to the experienced pet dealer. But so that you will know about it yourself, too: In

Guinea pigs recognize kin by scent. They touch noses to sniff and identify the other animal's body odor.

young males there's a noticeable distance between the genital opening and the opening of the anus. If you gently press the abdomen of the male with your thumb above the anal region, the penis will emerge. In the older male the testes are clearly recognizable as swellings to the right and left, alongside the anus. In females the genital organ is a long slit, which extends to the opening of the anus.

To determine sex, carefully press the guinea pig's belly near the anus. If it's a male, the penis will emerge.

What Breeds to Choose from

Guinea pigs are distinguished from one another mainly by their coat (see Breeds and Colors, page 47).

Smooth- or short-haired guinea pigs: These are slender, have a shining, smooth, close-lying coat, and are bred in many different colors (page 48).

Abyssinian guinea pigs: In these, because of a mutation, the hair grows in whorls or rosettes, which can ap-

pear anywhere on the body. For this reason the Abyssinian guinea pigs look very funny and somewhat shaggy, so that they are also called rough-haired (see Guinea Pigs with Special Hair Structure, page 49).

Long-haired or Angora guinea pigs: These have gorgeous, long, silky soft fur, up to 6 inches (15 cm) long, which requires intensive grooming so that it doesn't get snarled. There are cross-breeds in all colors and color combinations, just as with their short-haired relatives. The long-haired guinea pigs also occur in two varieties: the Peruvian guinea pig and the sheltie (page 50).

Advice for beginners: It's best if you buy one of the two breeds first mentioned. They present no problems either in housing or care.

Where Guinea Pigs Are to Be Found

Who hasn't stood spellbound before the window of a pet store with a guinea pig family burrowing around inside? Guinea pigs can also be found in the pet departments of large department stores, where they are available in many colors. If you think a rough-hair looks particularly sweet there, you can be sure you'll lose your heart to such an animal as you care for it later. This is especially true for children. If you have a special request, you'd best turn to the specific breeder. There may also be someone in your neighborhood who has some young guinea pigs to give away.

Five Buying Tips

1. It's best to try to pick out a young animal. These are clearly smaller than the fully grown and should be about five or six weeks old. A female that is older than two months may already be pregnant.

In the male (top) the distance between the genital opening and the anal opening is noticeably larger than in the female (bottom).

A roomy cage—even two or three guinea pigs will be comfortable in this.

2. Guinea pigs are social animals. So observe them carefully to see how the animal of your choice behaves toward its fellows. Sitting apathetically in a corner indicates illness.

3. Look at the coat. Much falling hair, thin fur, and bare spots are signs of illness or age.

4. Have the seller show you the guinea pig's teeth. Poor teeth position means difficulties to reckon with later (see Inspecting the Teeth, page 28)

5. Take some of the nest material from the display cage when you buy your animal. This helps the guinea pig get used to its new home.

Choosing the Right Guinea Pig
A healthy guinea pig has
• thick fur all over its body and is only hairless on the undersides of the feet and on the ears
• a compact body build
• a clean anal area

- clear eyes without discharges
- a dry nose

It is lively and active and "converses" with its fellow guinea pigs with various sounds.

An ailing guinea pig has a dull, unkempt coat. If in addition it has
- tearing, reddened, or swollen eyes and nostrils
- dirt in the ears
- small crusts around the mouth

it is not advisable to buy it.

My advice: If there is diarrhea (recognizable by the encrusted fur around the anal area), do not buy any other animal from the same cage. Diarrhea can be a sign of contagious bacterial or viral infection.

Providing for Vacation

When you are thinking of buying, you must also think about what provisions you can make for when you go on vacation. With enough water and dry food and hay, your guinea pigs can stay alone without any other arrangements for one to two days.

If you're going to be away longer, you can do one of the following things:

Take them with you: Since guinea pigs normally tolerate a journey and a change of climate well, they can be taken along in their cage or in a transport box. Protect them from drafts and strong sunlight on the journey! Ask beforehand if the hotel will accept you with your pets. If you are traveling abroad, find out from the consulate or veterinary office what formalities are necessary for crossing the border.

Give them to someone to take care of: Anyone who takes guinea pigs to relatives or friends should provide litter, hay, dry food, and a list of care procedures. Remember regular petting! Also remember to point out the dangers that can threaten such a

A raised platform serves as a lookout.

A rough stone helps to wear down claws.

small animal; otherwise, you may have the same experience we did.

We had taken our female guinea pigs Finni and Fanni to our neighbor, who had a balcony and intended to put the cage there. None of us, however, had thought about one thing: cats. So poor Finni fell victim to the orange-striped cat next door.

Most pet stores and boarding kennels will board guinea pigs. Call ahead of time, and find out if the animal can stay there in its own cage.

In the photos: *The right equipment. Guinea pigs like a thick layer of litter in their cage, a place to crawl under, and a raised area.*

9

Everything a Guinea Pig Needs

Guinea pigs have hardly any behavioral traits that require special living arrangements. They are not climbers and acrobats like hamsters; they can, of course, leap, but not as high as a rabbit. They also have no desire at all to "break out" of their pen. They thus present no great demands. But, all the same, it is still necessary to meet their requirements. Then they will stay healthy and lively and enjoy life with you.

Proper Guinea Pig Accommodations
Material: Plastic floor pan with metal caging on sides and top.
Size: At least 26½ × 14 × 13½ inches (68 × 36 × 35 cm).
Depth of floor pan: 4 to 6 inches (10 to 15 cm).
Mesh upper part: Able to be opened from side or top.
Alternatives: Plastic tub, homemade guinea pig cage (see page 11).

A Cage for a Feeling of Security
The pet shop offers guinea pig cages in different sizes and styles.
Good for a guinea pig is a cage with the dimensions 26½ × 14 × 13½ inches (68 × 36 × 35 cm), with a floor pan of plastic and a removable wire

cage above. The floor pan should be 4 to 6 inches (10 to 15 cm) deep, so that the litter, in which the guinea pig loves to worm around energetically, won't be so easily tossed out. If the cage opens at the side, the guinea pig can go in and out by itself at exercise time. If it opens from the top, it will be easier for you to put in the food and to clean the cage. Besides, it's easier to lift the animal out of the cage from above.

For two or more guinea pigs you need a correspondingly larger cage of at least 31 × 31 × 17½ inches (80 × 80 × 45 cm) or 39 × 15½ × 13½ inches (100 × 40 × 35 cm), so that the animals can have constant exercise and need to retreat into the cage only for eating and sleeping.

In this "landscape" of blocks and a wooden wagon, the young guinea pigs are able to chase tirelessly, run obstacle races, and play hide-and-seek.

Not recommended is a cage with a plastic removable hood with mesh for ventilation. Its only virtue is that it promotes tidiness (flying litter), but it isolates the guinea pig too much from its surroundings. Besides, terrific heat pressure can develop in plastic houses like this if, for instance, the sun should shine on the cage or it's placed too near the heat. Although guinea pigs come from tropical countries, they cannot tolerate so much heat.

Bad are cardboard boxes. They are soon soaked with urine and gnawed through. Wooden boxes without a special entryway cut into them (see illustration at right) are also not recommended. They are hard to clean and soak up urine, which smells unpleasant—especially in an apartment—and is unhygienic besides.

When guinea pigs are resting or sleeping, they lie on their belly and tuck their feet underneath their body. In this respect they differ from other rodents, who normally curl up.

A Plastic Tub as a Guinea Pig House

Many guinea pig owners use this alternative. It has advantages as well as disadvantages.

Advantages: It's cheaper to buy; the animal feels more secure; the litter can't be tossed out; the tub, which should be the size of a cage, is very easy to clean and wash out.

Disadvantages: The guinea pig can't see what's going on outside its quarters; hay racks and water bottles are difficult to fasten down; it isn't protected from dangers, such as cats, which could be life threatening.

My advice: Since your guinea pig needs a house to sleep in anyway (see page 14), the one can very easily be combined with the other. Put a wooden box—about 8 × 6 × 6 inches (20 × 15 × 15 cm)—inside the tub, with an exit hole cut in it, and fasten the hayrack and water bottle to it. Now if the guinea pig wants to see

something, it can jump on top of the little house and peer over the edge of the tub.

A Homemade Guinea Pig House

The pet store has prefabricated parts for the home builder that are very practical and easy to handle. However, if you want to do it yourself from scratch, you can allow your imagination free reign. Build your guinea pig a domicile that will provide it with a bit of what it has in the wild: hiding places, small hollows, a high place for a lookout, stones for sharpening its claws in a natural way, branches on which to gnaw. For instance, if you plan a second level, you provide your guinea pig with a double pleasure—a hiding place underneath and a lookout on top.

Important: Be sure to provide a removable bottom pan of tin or plastic, because wood, as I have already pointed out, is too likely to become soaked with urine.

As you plan, include the following considerations:
- Size: Like the ready-made cage, 26½ × 14 × 13½ inches (68 × 36 × 35 cm).

A simple wooden box with an entry hole cut into it will serve as a sleeping house. The guinea pig can retire there and even do a little gnawing.

11

Peruvian guinea pig in three colors.

Black Peruvian guinea pig.

Abyssinian guinea pig.

Wild guinea pig.

English and Abyssinian guinea pigs.

Different guinea pig breeds differ from each other chiefly in their fur and its colors. Besides the three best known breeds—English/American/Bolivian (smooth-haired), Abyssinian, and Peruvian guinea pigs—there are many other species and subspecies that are not so well known in the U.S.A. but are bred with great zeal in the Netherlands, Belgium, and England.

Abyssinian guinea pigs.

Abyssinian guinea pig.

Abyssinian guinea pig.

- Material: A 1-inch (20-mm) thick waterproof chipboard or wooden lattice.
- Platform: A third of the floor area at a height of about 6 inches (15 cm).
- Walls: Wire mesh, 13½ inches (35 cm) high on three sides and 9¾ inches (25 cm) on the fourth, the side with the platform on it. This side must be able to be opened so that you can remove the floor pan for cleaning.
- Equipment: A flat stone, which is laid in front of the platform so that the guinea pig will always run across it when it wants to jump up (see Cutting Claws, page 27); branches for gnawing and nibbling.

A Little House to Sleep in

Guinea pigs like to retreat into a little house to rest. This sleeping "with a roof over their head" goes back to the primordial life of guinea pigs, for they live in burrows in the wild. Use a wooden box for the sleeping house, its size depending on the size of the animal, and cut an entry hole in it. Or you can buy various house sizes in wood or plastic at the pet store. Wood is preferable to plastic in this case, so the guinea pig can sharpen his teeth on it. You will need to replace the house now and then during the life of the guinea pig.

I advise against closed plastic sleeping houses with floors. They don't "breathe," and the moisture in the guinea pig's exhaled breath condenses on the walls.

Tips for the do-it-yourselfer: You can easily make a house yourself if you observe the following rules:
- Don't use any plywood or fiber board, because the lime that these materials contain in great quantity is poisonous to the guinea pig. Natural wood, such as pine, fir, or larch, is more suitable. It is soft and easy to work with.
- Don't fasten the boards with wire staples; the guinea pig can injure itself by gnawing on them. Rather, use longer U-staples of steel, which can't be gnawed out so easily.
- If you glue the house, use a nontoxic glue. After gluing, allow to air for a few days. Reinforce the corners of the glued house with additional boards.

The Right Litter

Pet stores have special nontoxic litters (such as pine bedding) for small animals. These are very absorbent

The guinea pig feels best with "a roof over its head." Because it can protect itself in the wild only by hiding from its enemies, the sleeping house fits its natural behavior pattern.

and are free of toxic materials. To diminish odor, I recommend that you give the cage floor an underlayer of cat litter. Of course, there are also guinea pig keepers who recommend against this. They fear that the animals, especially young ones, will not only nibble on the hay and straw but also on the cat litter, and in time this will disagree with them. Observe carefully and do not use cat litter in such an instance.

Shopping List for Guinea Pig Equipment
Cage
Sleeping house
Two feed racks
Small animal litter
Food bowl
Drinking bottle
Straw, pine bedding
Maybe cat litter

Straw litter: Guinea pigs love this. They can rustle around in it, play hide-and-seek, and nibble on it. You can buy straw at the pet store.

Important: Get oat straw that has not been treated with growth inhibitors (chemical materials), which are toxic to guinea pigs. This straw isn't as absorbent as wheat straw and must be changed somewhat more often.

Feeding Racks

Two feeding racks should be provided in every cage. Usually they come with the cage, but they can also be bought from the pet store separately. One is for hay, the other for green feed, which should never be thrown into the cage, because it will be contaminated with droppings and urine. A snap lid of wood, with which the rack may be closed from above,

has proven to be very practical. The guinea pig will enjoy surveying the view from there. A cover like this is even advisable for young animals, because they so love to jump up everywhere that their little feet could get caught and injured in the rack.

Feeding Bowl and Water Bottle

Feeding bowl: It should be made of glazed clay or porcelain and be slightly narrower at the top. Then it will not tip over if the animal places its feet on it when eating, and the food will stay clean. Plastic dishes tip over easily, and guinea pigs don't like to look for their food in the litter.

Water bottle: For drinking water you'd best choose a gravity-flow bottle, which can be hung on the cage wire. The glass or plastic bottle should be furnished with a ball valve so that the water doesn't drip into the cage. The guinea pig will very quickly learn to get water from it drop by drop.

Every cage must have a hayrack. Put hay and greens there. Anything put on the cage floor will quickly become fouled with urine and droppings and will rot.

Guinea pigs quickly learn to drink from a gravity-flow water bottle. This way they can satisfy their thirst whenever they need to.

Two at the same dish makes the food taste better.

Drinking water in an open dish is not recommended; it's too easily contaminated by droppings and litter.

Combing and Brushing the Fur

Guinea pigs love to be gently combed and brushed from time to time. Depending on the breed, grooming may even be necessary. In addition, it fosters contact with the animal and serves to prevent encrustation and skin infections, thus promoting better health.

Smooth-haired guinea pigs need a medium-hard brush.

Abyssinian guinea pigs should be brushed lightly but also combed with a long-toothed comb.

Long-haired guinea pigs must be combed daily with a long-toothed comb. A soft brush will make the coat shine.

In the photos: *Varied diet. Guinea pigs that are well kept satisfy their hunger only as necessary. Animals that are constantly kept confined in a cage eat more than is good for them out of pure boredom.*

Clover is especially tasty. But the guinea pig shouldn't have too much.

Implements for Cage Cleaning

If you don't want to use cat litter (see page 14), urine stones may form in the cage corners. Since they will generate an unpleasant smell, you should have handy

- a brush
- a spatula
- a cleaning solution

Environmental tip: Don't use any strong chemical cleaning solution, only acetic acid or citric acid.

The Right Way to Handle Guinea Pigs

There is no more ideal pet for children than the guinea pig. It is sociable, not aggressive, loves to be petted and cuddled, and becomes more lively and alert the more it is talked to.

The Proper Place

Before you bring your guinea pig home, you should arrange its new quarters and choose a permanent place for them. There are a few things to take into consideration:

• The best place is a bright, not too warm, draft-free room, with no television or radio and also no smoking, if possible.

• Guinea pigs don't like noise and loud music; they are very timid. Besides, they have much better hearing than people and react negatively to sound waves that we can't even perceive.

• Drafts are harmful to them and are, in fact, one of the causes of their regrettably frequent respiratory illnesses. Therefore, do not place the cage on the floor but in a draft-free place on a sturdy table or a chest.

• Guinea pigs can't tolerate very much heat; therefore, do not place the cage in full sunlight or too close to the heating unit.

• Dark, damp cellar rooms are a torture for guinea pigs.

My advice: Since guinea pigs are ideal animals for children (see page 21), the cage will often be placed in a child's room. If there are friends visiting there and it may get noisy, consider removing the cage to another room. Otherwise the animal may become too frightened.

The New Home

It's best if you bring your guinea pig home in its little transport cage or in a basket as quickly as possible. The strange situation will surely frighten it, and even if it doesn't actually attempt to get away, you should still try to minimize the stress of moving as much as possible.

When you get home, put the transport box in the cage, open it, and let the guinea pig come out by itself. You shouldn't do anything more at first. A thick layer of hay, straw, or pine bedding will give the animal a chance to burrow in and observe everything from the calm of its secure hiding place. Then it will probably nibble a little of the hay and quell its first pangs of hunger. You can also help your guinea pig to learn trust in the following ways:

• The quieter it is around the cage, the more quickly the animal will get used to its new surroundings.

• Content yourself next with just putting fresh green feed in the rack and changing the water. Leave everything else in the cage the way it is; then your guinea pig will feel at home more quickly.

• Don't put the sleeping house in the cage ahead of time; wait until the guinea pig is hand tame. Otherwise it will always remain shy and keep itself in its hiding place.

• Children should tell friends who want to see their new house pet to wait until later.

How the Guinea Pig Gets Acclimated

Observation phase: For a while the guinea pig sits there quietly, surrounded by pine bedding, straw, or hay. It will nibble on it here and there, for this contributes to calming it, and it will also make its bed of hay. So it should also be able to observe its surroundings as much as possible, be in contact with them, as it were, so that it knows there is nothing threatening in its new environment. This can take hours, or sometimes even days, depending on how anxious the guinea pig is. You may need to explain this to your children if they are disappointed at this behavior after having been so excited about their new playmate.

Exploration phase: As soon as the animal comes creeping out curiously, you may talk gently to it. While doing so, keep using its name over and over again. When it no longer hides at the sound of your voice, you can carefully stroke it (see Hand Taming, below). When it also does not retreat at that, you can carefully take it out of the cage and set it down next to it. Finally, the guinea pig should also get to know the room where it will be living from now on. In doing so the guinea pig will certainly act as it does in the wild. Carefully it dares a few steps and then immediately seeks cover again. Watchful, it continues, turns around and runs, always on the same path, back to its cage. Then it trips off in a new direction. As in the wild, it actually lays down "beaten paths" from its cage; that is, it reconnoiters the room again and again from the same scampering trails in all directions.

My advice: Put a few treats for your guinea pig here and there; it will soon feel at home in its new surroundings.

Hand Taming

Since guinea pigs have been in the captivity of humans for so long, human presence—and human scent,

Keep giving your guinea pig treats from your hand. It will enjoy the attention and will repay you with trust and affection.

too—is no longer really strange to them. Young animals—that is, four- to six-week-old guinea pigs—still have plenty of natural instinct: they are shy and must first bond to their human through close contact. No guinea pig behaves exactly like the next. Some individuality can be clearly observed right from the beginning.

The first step: While speaking softly, offer the guinea pig a piece of carrot or apple. You must be patient, for it won't dare to take it right away but may snuffle a bit in that direction. It certainly won't bite your finger without warning (see How Guinea Pigs Communicate, page 54), as a hamster will, for instance, if it feels threatened. And sometime or other it will overcome its fear and take the treat out of your hand. Then the first ice is broken.

The second step: Now, since the guinea pig has gotten used to the scent of your hand and knows that only good comes from it, you can scratch its head gently. Because that's pleasant for it, it will sit there quietly,

Standing on hind legs for a treat.

Securing the treasure.

enjoying it. Now you can gently stroke its back; and when it no longer retreats at that, you will have won its trust.

The third step: Now the guinea pig is no longer likely to die of fright if you take it from its cage and set it in your lap. The length of time it takes to accomplish these three steps depends on the guinea pig. You must not lose patience. Explain this to your children, too. They can be sure that even the shyest guinea pig will in time be eating out of their hand and be the playmate they were expecting.

My advice: Always use a moderately soft voice when talking to the guinea pig, and also do not move suddenly. Otherwise the guinea pig will be frightened, and gaining its trust will take a long time.

When a Guinea Pig Can't Learn to Trust

There are only a few guinea pigs for whom the method described above is unsuccessful from the start. Perhaps these animals have undergone some experiences during the first weeks of their lives that have made them especially shy and anxious. Only one thing will help: the method of "gentle force." In this method you will have to deal with the fact that the guinea pig is a defenseless animal that in moments of danger "plays dead" when picked up.

Take the guinea pig on your lap again and again, stroke it, and speak reassuringly and gently to it. Give it its green feed or special treats only from your hand, and practice patience. The animal will slowly learn from experience that it has nothing to fear from

Sharing is better than fighting.

this human. Still, it will take much longer for you to win its trust.

With a guinea pig like this, you shouldn't put a sleeping house in the cage at first, but give it enough straw so that it can burrow into it. Then it has a feeling of protection, but it can't completely shut itself off from its surroundings.

The Correct Way to Pick Up and Carry

Since guinea pigs have very delicate limbs, you should never pick them up by the legs or hold them up at all. That produces the worst dislocations. Instead, grasp the animal with one hand underneath and then lift it up, supporting the rear end with the other hand. When you want to carry a

guinea pig around, set it on the palm of your hand or the crook of your arm, and keep it from falling with the other hand (see illustration page 22).

Children carry their guinea pig more securely if they hold it against the chest with both hands so that it can brace itself with its legs.

Guinea Pigs and Children

I know of no animal that is better suited for children than the guinea pig. It is sociable, loves to be petted and cuddled, and becomes livelier and more alert the more attention it gets. Thus guinea pigs are ideal for teaching children reasonable, natural behavior toward animals.

When the female guinea pigs Finni and Fanni came to live in our house-

In the photos:
Getting along with each other. It's part of the survival strategy of the guinea pig to join together in a herd, not take each other's food, never to scuffle or fight. Of course, they do observe very exact dominance ranking.

hold, my children were just six and seven years old. But they learned very quickly that these creatures had their own needs. Since feeding, watering, cleaning, and affection are simple jobs to accomplish, and the "payment"—a trusting animal—was not long in coming, they did their chores eagerly. They regularly collected greens and, with my help, cleaned the cage. But they applied themselves with special devotion to playing with their guinea pigs. I will never forget those buildings and landscapes of blocks, Lego, stones, and every other imaginable "building material," and the eagerly cooing and squeaking guinea pigs.

Carry the guinea pig by putting one hand under the belly to support it and grasping firmly with the other hand so that it doesn't fall.

My advice: Parents should keep an eye on the animals and share responsibility for them. Cast a look into the cage now and then to make sure that the guinea pig is still burrowing around in a lively way and is eating regularly. A changed behavior pattern usually indicates a health problem, which children might not be able to recognize right away.

Note: Many a guinea pig has been squeezed to death by young hands out of sheer love. It doesn't do anything to defend itself, doesn't bite, doesn't scratch, doesn't kick as hard as a rabbit, and cannot nimbly jump down like a cat. Make this very clear to your children to spare them the bitter experience of being responsible for the death of their pet.

Getting Along with Other Pets

By nature guinea pigs are not aggressive. They are fleeing animals only and are thus defenseless. For this reason you must not put them with animals that can be dangerous to them. There are always animal friendships that are the exception. You have to learn which ones through experience.

Dwarf rabbits usually provide the ideal domestic companionship for guinea pigs, since they get along very well together. The rabbits take over the protector's role for the guinea pigs; some animals even play together. But inevitably the rabbits bite their cage mates.

Dogs can be trained to accept guinea pigs as house mates, especially if both are young and acquired at the same time. But you shouldn't rely on the dog's training to ignore its hunting instinct when the guinea pig runs swiftly through the apartment.

Cats may regard the guinea pig as a prey animal and claw it, wound it badly, or even kill it. Or the two may get along well together. Nevertheless, I would never leave them alone together. There are always exceptions, of course, as the photograph on page 40 shows. If guinea pigs are going to be kept on a balcony or out of doors, they must always be protected from cats (see page 26).

Gerbils, deer mice, and hamsters do not get along with guinea pigs.

They speak another "language," and the guinea pig is not in a position to defend itself against the aggressiveness of these animals.

Parrots and large parakeets can be dangerous for guinea pigs. They easily become jealous, grab the animal, and may inflict severe injury with their powerful beaks. Therefore, don't ever leave these animals together unsupervised.

Housebreaking

Not every guinea pig can be house trained. Some animals learn quickly what to do and not to do outside their cage; with others it takes longer, and the younger the animal is, the better the prospects of success. The procedure is as follows:

• Observe whether the guinea pig has a particular favorite corner, and place a shallow plastic dish filled with cat or cage litter there.
• Keep putting the guinea pig on it.
• If it has gone somewhere else, collect the droppings, place them in the dish, and set the guinea pig on it.
• Each time it uses the toilet, reward the guinea pig with a treat.

My advice: If the animal has the free run of the apartment, place one of these toilets in each room.

Eating droppings: Many guinea pig keepers who see their animals doing this consider it unappetizing or unnatural. Still, eating their caecal excrement—for that is what it is—is a necessity of life. Guinea pigs form vitamins of the B complex in the appendix and supply themselves with it through the eating of these droppings, which are lighter and softer than the normal fecal pellet.

Exercise in the House

Guinea pigs are extremely lively animals. In spite of their plump bodies, they move skillfully and nimbly, run wild escape races, and contrive obstacle races. You must offer your animal the chance to do this. Only when it is able to train its bodily and mental capabilities can it show you its broad range of expression and behavior patterns. And isn't that what you want from companionship with a guinea pig?

Children carry their guinea pig more securely by holding it against the chest with both hands so that it can brace itself with all four feet.

A guinea pig needs devotion, which can be expressed in many ways. It likes to be petted or combed and brushed, especially at shedding time. And if you play with it, you promote its physical and mental capabilities.

What to watch out for during exercise:
• There should be no valuable carpets and furniture in the room, for they can be gnawed and soiled.
• Electric wires should not be within reach. Guinea pigs love to gnaw on them, and that can sometimes be fatal. Telephone wires are not immune either.
• Place a shallow dish with litter in the room for a guinea pig toilet.

- Don't leave newspapers or books lying around. Guinea pigs are regular rascals and love to work on paper especially. Even wallpaper can be chewed.
- Provide an environment with plenty of variety, with corners, niches, raised places (overturned flowerpots), or little obstacles to be jumped over.

Summer Outdoors on the Balcony

If you have a balcony, let your guinea pig share it with you. Arrange its home there so that it can enjoy life from spring until late fall. The animal must be taken indoors when the external temperature falls below 50 °F (10°C). You should also observe the following:

Security: Most balcony railings would not keep a guinea pig from slipping through and falling to its death. Reinforce the balcony grill with wire mesh, which should go from the floor to about 20 inches (50 cm) high. Or enclose the railing with planks, and then the guinea pig will also be protected from drafts.

Protection: The balcony should be protected against wind, rain, and strong sunlight. Cover the cold cement floor with old carpet pieces or a natural grass mat, so that the guinea pig doesn't get cold.

Cats: The guinea pig should not be left unattended on a balcony on the ground floor that is accessible to cats (see page 22). If this is not possible, secure the balcony with fine screening.

Body training is important, or alert, lively animals will turn into stiff, sluggish barrels.

Temperature change: When changing from the inside to the outside or vice versa, you must get the guinea pig used to the new temperature; otherwise it will catch cold. At first set it out in the warm midday hours and bring it in again at night. In the fall don't bring it into a heated room right away. The guinea pig feels best at temperatures of 64 to 68°F (18 to 20°C).

Feeding: The guinea pig on the balcony must receive fresh food and water twice daily.

Overnight: For this the animal needs its sleeping house (see page 14).

Furthermore, don't forget the dish with litter for a toilet.

A Guinea Pig Home in the Yard

If you have a yard, you can provide regular exercise for your animal or even set up permanent quarters. If you want to keep several animals and establish a guinea pig family, an outdoor pen is ideal, provided it's large enough. Bonding to humans isn't so close then, since life with the group satisfies the animals completely (see Communal Life in the Herd, page 53).

The Pen: Ready-made collapsible pens are available from the pet store. But you can also build one yourself. Using a framework of 1½ × 1½ inch lumber, the floor, sides, and roof of the hutch can be constructed with ¾-inch tongue-and-groove strips. Outdoor hutches should have a roof that slants down toward the back and be covered with a waterproof material. The front of the hutch can be covered with either ½- or 1-inch wire mesh.

The walls of the pen should be at least 12 inches (31 cm) high. The pen should not be smaller than 1 square yard (1 m²) in area. A roof of wire mesh is also needed, so that the defenseless guinea pigs are not threat-

The teeth meet exactly and can wear each other down naturally.

Incisors that don't wear themselves down curl inward like horns and prevent the animal from eating.

ened from above by cats, dogs, martens, or birds of prey.

Security: The runway needn't necessarily be anchored in the ground, since guinea pigs dig very little. But it should stand on level ground, so that the animals can't slip out and rats and weasels can't slip in.

Shelter: Guinea pigs need a shelter in their pen not only as protection from rain, sun, and wind, but also as a retreat from enemies, or if they are frightened. It should be at least as large as the cage in the house: about 27 × 16 × 13½ inches (70 × 40 × 35 cm). Several guinea pigs, of course, need a correspondingly larger house.

It should be made of ¾-inch (20-mm) thick waterproof chipboard or natural wood lath, with a solid floor, a window, and a removable or hinged roof; otherwise the old straw can't be removed. Cut a large entrance hole in the front, about 4 to 6 inches (10 to 15 cm) in size, and close it with a slide or a flap, or hang a burlap sack over it. Cover the roof with tar paper, make it steeper on the weather side, and let it extend far enough so that the feeding and drinking bowls can be placed under it and protected from the weather. Attach one or two hay racks inside the house.

My advice: Paint the house with a

To keep the house from smelling of guinea pigs, first put a layer of odor-absorbent cat litter in the cage tray, and then spread a thick layer of small animal litter or wood shavings and straw over it. Guinea pig feet are quite tender and can be injured by the hard little stones of cat litter.

A guinea pig herd is best housed in an outside pen. Find a shady place under a tree and provide a shelter, so that the animals can go inside in bad weather.

nontoxic wood preservative to protect it from dampness and parasites. Lead-based paints must not be used for interiors.

Grooming

A healthy guinea pig grooms and cleans itself regularly and thoroughly. Still, it also likes to be combed and brushed gently and lovingly. Aside from the fact that brushing helps keep the animal clean and offers a good skin massage, it also means that you give your pet attention as you take care of it. In addition, during grooming you have a chance to discover parasites and skin disease in time. The various guinea pig breeds have the following specific needs:

Guinea pigs groom themselves regularly and thoroughly. They lick their fur with their tongue and remove the dust and loose fur with their claws.

A comb and brush for the daily grooming of the coat, which is essential in the case of Peruvian guinea pigs.

Short-haired and Abyssinian guinea pigs: You need to groom daily only during the shedding season, usually in spring and fall, because it removes the dead hair from the coat.

Peruvian guinea pigs: Daily grooming is a must, since they can have hair up to 8 inches (20 cm) long. Otherwise the fur will mat, and urine and feces will be trapped in it.

Get your guinea pig accustomed to grooming when it's young, even if its coat is not yet fully developed.

This is how it's done:
• Don't place the animal directly on the cold table while it's being groomed. Always put a warm cloth under it.
• Give it a treat as a reward, stroking and talking gently to it.
• A long-toothed comb serves for disentangling the hair; a soft brush brings out the shine.
• Wash out and comb sticky places in the fur, especially at the rear end; cutting may be necessary ultimately.
• Bathe only if absolutely necessary, in lukewarm water, using a mild baby shampoo. Carefully dry the guinea pig and protect if from any draft, since the danger of catching cold is especially great.

Cutting Claws

Regular examination is needed. Claws that are too long interfere with the animal's movement because it can't put its feet down properly any longer. If the claws don't get worn down by natural means—for instance, on rough ground (see page 14)—they grow too long. To avoid crippling or infection, the claws must be cut with special clippers by a pet dealer or a

"Washing" its face with a foot.

Licking its belly.

Scratching under its chin.

veterinarian. You can have them sho
you, too, but be careful! Blood vesse
and nerve endings, which can be
seen only moderately well even in
light-colored claws, must not be injured. That causes the animal great
pain.

Inspecting the Teeth

Since the teeth of the guinea pig
are constantly growing, they must be
worn down with hard food—for exam
ple, old bread, gnawing rolls, or gnaw
ing sticks (both available from a pet
store)—or with branches in the natur
manner.

Congenital dental malformation:
Unfortunately, this occurs often in
guinea pigs. The incisors do not mee
and rub against each other in such a
way that they are worn down by constant gnawing, and they continue to
grow. Regular shortening, which only
a veterinarian can undertake, is then
necessary every two to three months

A Clean Guinea Pig Home

Litter: Change once a week and
put in the barrel for compostable trasl
(if available). Those who have gar-
dens can throw shavings, pine bedding, or straw on their compost heaps
Cat litter goes in the garbage can.

Plastic floor trays: Clean thoroughly with warm water and mild
household cleaner. Loosen calcified
urine with acetic or citric acid, and remove with a spatula or brush. Do not
use any strong cleaning material,
since it could have a caustic effect on
the skin and mucous membranes of
the animals. Disinfection is necessary
only in case of sickness.

Food containers and water bottle
If possible rinse every two days under
clear running water. Scrub out the
drinking bottle with a bottle brush, so
that no algae will develop in it.

Dangers for Guinea Pigs

Danger	Source of Danger	Avoiding the Danger
Falling	Balcony	Secure with wire mesh or boards.
	Table	Do not let animals run free without supervision.
Pinching	Doors	Do not open and close without looking.
Heat stroke	Sun, heating units	Never let the cage stand in direct sunlight or near the heating unit.
Electric shock	Electric wires	Place wires under trim; do not leave cords lying around; pull plugs during exercise period.
Burns	Hot objects	Do not allow animals to run in the vicinity of stove or toaster.
Poison	Many plants, such as African violets, azaleas, dieffenbachia, ivy, oleander, poinsettia; ask at the florist or look up in the literature.	Do not have poisonous plants in the guinea pig's environment.
	Stained and lacquered wood	Use nontoxic material.
Injuries	Human feet	Be careful when guinea pig is loose.

Body care is important. Since the guinea pig comes into the world with a completely developed coat, you can begin to groom it soon after birth. This great independence, which includes other capabilities, is necessary for survival.

Proper Diet

As the famous animal researcher Alfred Brehm wrote, guinea pigs are easy to keep. "They eat various plant foods, from the roots to the leaves, grains as well as fresh, juicy plants, and require only some variety in their diet."

It is, therefore, not difficult to feed the animals. Still guinea pigs do have certain requirements for protein, carbohydrates, fats, fiber, minerals, and vitamins, which should be precisely balanced. The more variety the better. In addition to a proper diet, they need exercise on a continual basis. Animals that are always confined to a cage often eat more than is good for them out of boredom. If they get enough exercise, they satisfy their hunger according to need alone.

Many plants, such as dandelion, are suitable as green feed. Don't pick them near highly traveled roads (lead poisoning) or from fields where dogs run (transmission of illness through dog feces).

Hay, the Basic Food

Hay is as important to the guinea pig as bread is to us. In winter a guinea pig can live exclusively on hay and water, if no fresh green leaf vegetables are available. In the pet store hay comes packed in small bundles. You can buy larger quantities from a farmer.

When buying, keep in mind the following:
- Good hay contains cuttings of young grasses, clover, and weeds. This hay has an aromatic smell and a light green color.
- "Second cut" refers to hay from the second harvest in the same season.
- Poor hay is either too old or lacks the valuable weeds. Old hay is dusty, which makes the guinea pigs sneeze.

Yellowish hay consists of dried out, woody grasses, which are not nourishing to the guinea pig. The animal can die from rotten or moldy hay.

Besides meadow hay, the guinea pig also likes to eat clover and alfalfa hay, bean and pea straw, and especially hay made from stinging nettles, which contains many nutrients and promotes a beautiful coat. The stinging nettle, so hated and battled by many gardeners as a pesky weed, is rich in calcium, iron, phosphorus, and protein. In addition, it is high in vitamin D, which is important for bone building and promotes blood purification and metabolism. You can also offer your guinea pig the fresh plant, but let it wilt a bit first so that it doesn't sting so.

Homemade stinging nettle hay: Cut young plants without flowers (old plants sting too much) and dry them outdoors for three to four days, but don't let them dry in direct sunlight. Turn the hay twice daily during this period. Hang in bunches in a shady, well-ventilated place.

Green, Juicy Food

This is the most natural and healthiest food for a guinea pig. Food plants, vegetables, and fruit have a high nutrient content and are rich in protein, calcium, and vitamin C, which the guinea pig (alone among the rodents) cannot synthesize itself.

Good food plants to gather: Dandelion leaves (in spring), also flowers and seed heads, grass, colt's foot, meadow horsetail, chickweed, yarrow, comfrey, hogweed, plantain, and many more. Collect only plants that you can identify for certain! Use a plant guide if necessary.

Excellent: Clover. Since it is very gassy, mix in small amounts only.

Poisonous: Autumn crocus, fool's parsley, hemlock (not the evergreen tree, but an herb of the carrot family), elderberry, toadflax, foxglove, buttercup, ragwort, deadly nightshade (belladonna), black nightshade, laburnum, yew plants, and many others.

Do not pick plants

• along the edge of much-traveled roads and in the vicinity of freeways (lead poisoning!)
• in fields that have been treated with chemicals
• in parks and on lawns where many dogs have been walked, since disease can be transmitted by their feces and urine

Good food from kitchen and garden: Apples, bananas, pears, strawberries, grapefruit, honeydew melon, kiwis, tangerines, yellow plums, oranges, watermelon, grapes, lemons, cauliflower leaves, broccoli, all salad vegetables (except iceberg lettuce), turnips, potatoes (peeled), kohlrabi, peppers, parsley, red beets, cucumber, celery, spinach, tomatoes, and zucchini.

Not so good: Iceberg lettuce, especially if it comes from a greenhouse (loaded with nitrates), and all varieties of green cabbage since these usually cause flatulence. Feed Chinese cabbage, cauliflower, and red cabbage in very small quantities.

Poisonous: Potato peelings and raw beans.

My advice: Sow grass or lettuce seeds in a pot and you will always have healthy, fresh food for your guinea pigs. Packages already planted with grass seeds are available in the pet store as the so-called cat grass.

Ready-Mixed Feed

This is offered as concentrated food for guinea pigs in pet stores and in the pet departments of large department stores. This feed contains wheat, oats, corn, peanuts, sunflower seeds, as well as pellets. The pellets are made of compressed hay with vitamins and minerals added; they can also serve as the sole feed if you are away for one to two days.

One to two tablespoons daily per guinea pig is enough; otherwise the animal will get too fat. If it's fed much greenery at the same time, you can offer even less of the concentrated food.

Warning: Some guinea pigs are mad for corn feed. Don't let yourself be seduced by their begging and squeaking. An animal that is too fat dies young.

As a rule, guinea pigs enjoy using a salt lick. This is a good way to avoid a deficiency of minerals and trace elements.

Food for Gnawing

Guinea pigs need food to gnaw on so that they can wear down their constantly growing teeth (see page 28). Hard bread is good, but it mustn't be moldy, spiced, or salty. The pet store offers a variety of crackers, nibbling hearts, and sticks in all kinds of fla-

vors. Now and then put some branches (birch, willow, or fruit tree) in the cage for the animals to gnaw on.

Important: Don't give them any sprayed or frozen branches!

Drinking Water Is Important

Since guinea pigs don't drink much; many people think they need almost no water at all. This is not true, however. Always have water for your guinea pigs, and let them decide for themselves when and how much to drink. The gravity-flow bottle, which must be filled with fresh water daily, must always be available in the cage. Please use only settled or boiled water, since the chlorinated water directly from the faucet is bad for the animals.

Milk is food—not drink. Now and then you can give them milk that has been thinned with water. But be cautious. Don't let milk stand, since it quickly becomes sour. Guinea pigs can also get diarrhea from milk.

Vitamins and Minerals

A salt lick offers the guinea pig the necessary salt in an adequate ratio of components. Not every animal will like it, but it should be available just in case. Hang it on the cage wire; on the floor the stone will soak up urine.

Vitamin preparations are available from the pet store. With a healthy and varied diet, especially one rich in vitamin C, they are not really necessary, but dispensing one a week will give you the assurance that your guinea pig is sufficiently provided with all the necessities.

Greens are the guinea pig's favorite food. When they get them out of the pot themselves, they're always fresh.

A female guinea pig will occasionally show her teeth, but only in order to deter an importunate male. Otherwise guinea pigs are very peaceable and only open their mouths to yawn.

Earth is good for the guinea pig, so long as it's unpoisoned and free of pesticides. Tests have shown that well-rotted garden compost can also be a valuable food additive.

Ten Golden Rules for Feeding

1. Always feed at the same hour. The guinea pigs get used to it.

2. Never give too much at once. Take out of the cage whatever is not eaten after one hour. (This doesn't apply to hay.) The animal keeps eating from a dish that is constantly filled only out of boredom, gets too fat, and, as a result, gets sick.

3. Only fresh food is really good. Greens, vegetables, and fruit should not be wilted, rotten, or moldy.

4. Always put hay and greens in the rack. Don't throw them on the floor of the cage. They will be fouled by droppings and urine there.

5. Always wash fruit and vegetables thoroughly, rinse, and dry. Kitchen vegetable and fruit peelings should also be washed.

6. Don't feed directly from the refrigerator.

7. Daily refill the drinking bottle

Fresh fruit and vegetables are the correct juicy feed for guinea pigs. Make sure that it isn't dirty, rotten, or moldy, and remember that it may have been treated with chemicals. So wash thoroughly and peel!

with water that has been boiled or allowed to stand.

8. Every now and then put a willow, fruit tree branch (not sprayed!), or old bread into the cage for gnawing and nibbling.

9. Guinea pigs like to eat out of your hand and let themselves be stroked while they are doing it. So it's good for the friendship between human and animal if you take enough time for feeding and give special treats by hand (for instance a dandelion leaf or a couple of peanuts).

10. Provide enough exercise so that your guinea pigs remain vital and healthy. If they've put on fat, calmly institute one fast day per week, during which only hay and water are provided.

The gnawing stick, which the guinea pig uses to wear down its teeth naturally, can be purchased at the pet store.

Suggested Feeding Schedule

Time	Food	Quantity
Morning	Concentrated feed	0.7 ounce (20 g) 1–2 tablespoons)
	Juicy feed	1–2 lettuce leaves 1 small carrot or red beet 1 apple quarter
Afternoon or early evening	Greens	1 rack full of fresh grass, clover, dandelion leaves, colt's foot, young stinging nettles, and other plants.
Daily	Hay	Put in the rack the amount the animal will eat in a day.
Once a week	Gnawing food, such as old bread	½ ounce (15 g)
	Branches and (in the fall) dried leaves	As desired

What to Do When Your Guinea Pig Gets Sick

Prevention Is Better than Cure

Guinea pigs are not very hardy animals by nature. If they are kept properly, receive a good, varied diet, and get enough exercise, that is their best protection against illness. When illnesses do occur, it's usually because of poor nutrition or too little opportunity for movement. With a diet that is too rich, agile and lively animals turn into fat, sluggish little barrels who suffer an early death.

Hygiene is important: Bacteria, viruses, and parasites can be transmitted to guinea pigs from other pets or people. Spoiled food is the cause of intestinal ailments. Human beings can get skin fungus infections from close contact with guinea pigs. Therefore, wash your hands after playing with and caring for your pets. In principle, no animal should ever be kissed or held to the face.

My advice: Tell your child that too much close petting can result in his infecting the guinea pig with something. This argument may be more persuasive than warnings and prohibitions.

Maintenance mistakes that can cause sickness:
- bad food
- unbalanced diet
- drafts
- quick change from cold to heat or vice versa
- too high or too low humidity
- damp litter
- not enough exercise
- keeping together several animals that do not tolerate each other (stress)

What You Can Do Right Away

As an animal keeper you have the responsibility to recognize the first signs of illness in time and to do something (see Checklist of Ailments and Illnesses, page 39). With indispositions and simple health disorders it's often enough to remove the cause to get the guinea pig running around briskly once again. But bear in mind that so small a creature needs quick and effective help, and do not try to take the place of the veterinarian.

Sometimes it's necessary to give a guinea pig medicine. Grasp the animal securely by its back and introduce the eyedropper sideways behind the incisors.

Health Examination

	Healthy Guinea Pig	Sick Guinea Pig
Eyes	Bright, without discharge	Inflamed, sticky
Nose	Dry	Crusted, discharge
Coat	Shining, clean	Thin, dull, with bare spots
Anal area	Clean	Smeared with feces
Body shape	Plump	Flanks caved in
Behavior	Alert, lively	Dull, apathetic

Chemicals help against parasites or skin fungus, which can be a severe problem for an animal; apply with a cotton swab on the affected spot or behind the ear.

However, there are one or two things you can do yourself.
Treatment for mild diarrhea (if accompanied by loss of appetite, go to the veterinarian immediately): Change the litter more often and provide warmth. Offer lukewarm chamomile or fennel tea with grated carrot or apple. The diarrhea should disappear after two days at the most. Otherwise go to the veterinarian.

Treatment for mild constipation: Provide much water and exercise, with a teaspoon of olive oil in addition. If no improvement occurs after 24 hours, get advice from the veterinarian.

Treatment for inflamed nose: Eliminate the cause (for instance, dusty hay or strong cleaning materials that give off gases). In case of doubt, go to the veterinarian.

Standing on its hind legs is a difficult balancing act for a guinea pig.

Feeding is simple and inexpensive. Guinea pigs are vegetarians and can be fed, as they are in the wild, on fresh and dried plant parts. Many of these can be found in the garden or brought home from a walk.

First aid for heat stroke: If you observe that the guinea pig runs excitedly back and forth, at the same time panting and trembling all over, put the animal in the shade at once and offer it room-temperature water. Carefully dip its limbs in cool (not cold) water. Wrap cool, damp cloths closely around the body and calm the animal with gentle words and loving stroking.

The Trip to the Veterinarian

Guinea pigs are docile patients that scarcely utter a cry of pain. Do not defer the visit to the veterinarian for too long. It's best to take the animal to the clinic in a well-fastened little basket or in an animal transport container (pet store). Please don't take it out of the container and set it on your lap in the waiting room. The guinea pig can jump down in sheer terror and thus injure itself. Help the veterinarian by having the following information ready:
- When was the first time you noticed a change in behavior?

- When, how much, and what did it eat?
- How do the droppings look? Bring a fecal sample.
- How old is the animal?
- Is it kept with other guinea pigs or were any other guinea pigs or other pets visiting lately?
- Have there been any other changes (for instance, cage location, diet, a new guinea pig)?

Tips for Care

- Maintain meticulous cleanliness in the cage. During infectious illnesses, change litter often. Disinfect cage and all its contents (for instance, with Lysol, diluted 4 ounces per gallon of water).
- Provide quiet in the vicinity of the cage. Avoid swings of temperature, drafts, and other stresses.
- Separate the animal from other guinea pigs into its own cage, preferably in another room, at the first sign of illness.
- Follow the doctor's orders precisely, and give the medications as prescribed.
- Do not lose patience and become neglectful if the treatment goes on for a while.

Putting to Sleep

If the guinea pig is suffering from a painful and untreatable illness, it's sometimes better to put the animal to sleep. Obviously only the veterinarian can decide whether it's advisable.

When our guinea pig Finni fell victim to a cat, her companion Fanni suffered such a shock that she would no longer eat. One day she, too, lay dead in her cage. But since I had already prepared my children for it and we had spoken about whether we should shorten her suffering, her death did not seem quite so painful to them.

The guinea pig is a toe walker; on its front feet (top) it has four toes with claws, and three on its hind feet (bottom). Since the claws are wide, it is also called "hoof-footed."

The guinea pig's claws can't be worn down naturally, because it hasn't the chance to do enough running over rough ground, and must be trimmed regularly. But don't cut them too short, because that will injure the animal.

Checklist of Ailments and Illnesses

Symptom	Possible Causes Often Curable at Home	Possible Diagnosis Needing Prompt Treatment by Veterinarian
Sits around listlessly	Boredom	Anything unknown, possible infection
Doesn't eat	Environment too cool and damp, overheating, draft, not enough to gnaw	Anything possible; teeth too long, possible malocclusion
Drooling	Possibly not enough to gnaw	Teeth too long, virus infection, malocclusion
Diarrhea	Bad food, draft, environment too cool or too damp	Worm infestation (very rare), bacterial infection
Straining without producing feces and urine	Too little exercise, poor nutrition	Constipation, kidney and bladder inflammation, virus infection
Sneezing, throat rattling	Draft, temperatures too low or too high, air too dry or too damp	Viral or bacterial infection
Rapid breathing	Panting with great heat, shock, fear, stress	Heat stroke
Scratching	Unclean maintenance, bad grooming	Parasites (mites), skin fungus, skin inflammation
Limping	Environment too damp, lack of exercise, overweight	Abscess on ball of foot
Slight bleeding	Wounds from fighting with rival	For mild wounds apply iodine, for severe ones go to veterinarian
Bare spots in fur	Inadequate diet	Deficiency diseases, sometimes fungal skin disease

When Guinea Pigs Have Babies

Surprise Offspring

Many guinea pig owners have had the following experience: Convinced that they had a male, they are amazed that, in spite of following the feeding rules exactly, the animal kept getting plumper. But they didn't think anything was amiss until they looked in the cage one morning and found four guinea pigs instead of one. Such surprise offspring can also materialize when children take their guinea pigs, whose sex is unknown, to visit other guinea pig owners. You need not be unhappy about such surprise offspring, for a guinea pig nursery is charming, but you do need to provide accommodations for the young fairly soon. In five to six weeks the females will become fertile again, and this multiplication can proceed without letup.

How the Pair Lives Together

There are two reasons for deciding to have a pair:
• interest and pleasure in keeping a pair, birth, and the raising of the young
• developing different breeds and color types

Getting them used to each other: If you want to put a second guinea pig

with the one you already have, it's advisable to get them used to each other first. This also applies to two females or two castrated males (see Male or Female? page 6). A prerequisite is a cage large enough (at least 31 × 31 × 17½ inches (80 × 80 × 45 cm), which is divided through the middle by a mesh sliding partition. This allows both animals to see each other and also sniff. After one to two days, you should take the partition out and let the two guinea pigs be together under your watchful eye. At first they may try to dominate and to push each other. That's normal. But if they bite, you must separate them and try to introduce them again after a while. However, if the animals still don't get along, you must try a different pair.

My advice: Rub your hands with perfume and stroke the guinea pigs thoroughly. This will temporarily suppress the animals' scent, and they will live peacefully together.

Living together: As a rule, the male and the female live together amicably. The boar (as the male is called) behaves peacefully toward the female (the sow), and she always defers to him. To protect herself against his advances, the sow gives her partner "a rap on the knuckles" with her teeth or sometimes pulls out a few of his neck hairs. The male not only endures all this patiently, but also leaves special treats for the female, whereas two females or two males will often fight over them obstinately.

Did you know that the guinea pig young open their eyes in the mother's womb 14 days before they are born? And that they have teeth with which they can start nibbling on grass and hay blades a few hours after they are born?

A close friendship like this between guinea pigs and cats occurs only rarely.

Courtship

It is moving to watch how persistently the male tries to win the favor of the female. Again and again he circles his lady with slow steps and wagging rear end and makes chattering sounds. At the same time, he tries to slide his body along that of the female. At first he is shoved away. The female sits up on her hind legs, straightens her knees, and, with her jaws wide open, shows her teeth. If this warning isn't enough, she may run her teeth over the suitor's nose. The male then withdraws with a squeak. When they know each other better, the female merely moves out of the male's way or lets out a few sprays of urine in order to put him in his place. The male is "given a favorable hearing" only if the female is in estrus, that is, ready to mate.

Mating

This happens every 14 to 18 days, when the eggs that have developed in the ovaries are in the right phase for fertilization. The vagina, which is usually closed by a mucus plug, is clear for 24 hours. The female is now ready for mating. She lies on her belly, with her rear end raised.

Copulation lasts only a few seconds. Afterward both animals clean themselves conspicuously and carefully, especially in the genital region.

Pregnancy

Pregnancy lasts approximately eight to ten weeks. Usually it is so uncomplicated that you won't notice any changes in the behavior of the animal. Large litters have a shorter gestation than small ones. During this period the male is very attentive and gives the mother-to-be the best place at the feeding dish. After about four weeks, the female grows fatter; in the last two weeks of the pregnancy she is decidedly plump. This is no wonder, since the young comprise more than half of her own weight. You can clearly see their movements in the mother's body and also feel them. The female doesn't make any nest-building preparations or behave in any unusual way, which is why an inexperienced guinea pig owner often doesn't have any idea of what is about to happen.

Male and female first sniff each other thoroughly. This way they establish very quickly whether they like each other. But this contact sniffing is not actually a part of the courtship ritual.

Should the Male Be Present at the Birth?

Usually the sow is indifferent as to whether the boar is present. But he can also have a calming effect on the mother. There have been cases in which the father has helped to lick the newborn babies dry. In general, however, he seems to be indifferent to the proceedings and usually stays at the other end of the cage.

My advice: Remove the boar before the birth. The female will come into estrus again several hours later and will let the boar mate. Then new young may be expected about two months later. After three to four days you can let the boar return to his family (see Family Life, page 46).

Birth

Birth frequently occurs in the daytime, and it can be a suspenseful and exciting event to behold, especially for children. Like everything else about guinea pigs, this experience is entirely uncomplicated. The expectant mother just sits there and nibbles happily on a blade of grass. The birth of her young begins suddenly and is over after a quarter of an hour. Since the animal is not disturbed by onlookers, you can in good conscience allow your children to observe. Hectic excitement, however, should be avoided.

Course of birth: The female remains sitting, and the young come out underneath. She pulls off the sac backwards between her forelegs and eats it. This is important, otherwise the young would soon suffocate. Afterward the mother licks the newborn's mouth, nose, and eyes clean. One newborn is barely taken care of when the next one appears. At the end of the birth process some blood appears, along with the afterbirth (placenta), which is entirely or partly eaten by the mother.

Guinea pigs are born with eyes open and a full coat of fur. The birth weight ranges between 1½ and 3½ ounces (40 and 100 g).

It's a lot of fun to observe the family life of the guinea pig. They do everything together. They eat together, groom each other, cuddle with each other, and have—so it appears—a great deal to tell one another.

Newborn and Already Independent

Guinea pigs come into the world completely developed. Their eyes are open (and have been for 14 days in the mother's womb) and their fur is thick and silky. They are, in fact, precocial; that is, they can run and eat grass, hay, and other solid food, for they are born with permanent teeth. Two hours after birth the young begin to burrow in the cage in a lively way, though they still stay in the vicinity of their mother and will be nursing for two to three weeks. In addition to nursing, they nibble on feed and hay, so that it's not very difficult to raise orphaned guinea pig young.

If the young are orphaned, you may offer as a substitute for mother's milk

In the photos:
Guinea pigs are precocial. Very soon after birth the babies take a little solid food. So there's no fighting on the milk line. Each patiently awaits its turn.

Standing on the milk line.

- baby food for puppies (pet store)
- mashed peeled garden cucumbers
- grated apple
- oat flakes
- chopped bread
- pureed carrots (baby food)
- greens such as lettuce (unsprayed!) and dandelions

Not recommended is milk, whether thinned cow's milk or canned milk. If the babies are unable to feed themselves, feed them with a syringe (without the needle!) or a small bottle.

My advice: Check around in your neighborhood to see if there's another guinea pig that has just given birth, and put your little orphan with it. This usually works well. In the wild, where the animals live together in herds, the young nurse with other nursing females and are not nursed only by their own mother (see page 53).

How Often Should the Female Mate?

As has been noted before, the guinea pig female is ready to mate again immediately after giving birth. Allowing nature to run its course freely, however, can only be of interest to those who don't care how long the animals live. Give the mother a rest period between pregnancies. You'll be able to see for yourself whether she was weakened by the last litter. Let her get herself back together and mate only when the young are five to six weeks old—that is, ready to give away.

Lettuce tastes good too.

Note: Remember that the problems of multiplication are related to the early sexual maturity of guinea pigs. If you want to inhibit production of more young, you must separate the animals by sex. Females get along peacefully with one another. Males, on the other hand, begin to fight for dominance with the onset of sexual maturity.

Inbreeding: If the animals of one family mate with one another over generations, the danger of malformations arises (for example, missing eyes, crippled feet, defects of the inner organs, diminished life expectancy). Therefore, inbreeding, (for instance, between mother and son or father and daughter) to develop certain colors or markings should never continue over several generations.

The Development of the Young

Birth weight:	1 to 3½ ounces (40 to 100 g).
Full grown:	Male up to 63 ounces (1800 g); female up to 38½ ounces (1100 g).
Feed:	Mother's milk, to which are added solid foods like hay, lettuce, dandelion, oat flakes, apple pieces, bread cubes, prepared feed.
Independent:	At five weeks.
Sexually mature:	Female at five to six weeks, male at nine to ten weeks.

Family Life

A guinea pig family lives peacefully and closely together. The mother nurses her young regularly. She has only two teats, but since the young eat solid food by themselves, there is no quarreling at the milk source. Each one patiently awaits its turn. The babies follow the father as well as the mother. The family does everything together They eat together, clean themselves, cuddle one another, and—it appears—have much to tell each other. At exercise time they march in a line like geese. If a small one should get lost and squeak, the mother or the father runs over to it and leads it with gentle cooing back to the other young (see page 53).

You can watch the babies for hours. Even on the day they are born they begin to hop. They leap straight up in the air with all four feet and double back while still in the air. They run after each other, flit into the sleeping house and out again, perform the wildest goat leaps, and jump over barriers with such ease that you can only marvel and rejoice at it. With the onset of sexual maturity this playfulness abates, but you can retain these high spirits in your guinea pig. Give it much exercise and activity (see Exercise in the House, page 23) and feed it the right food in the proper amounts, and your grown-up pet will still charm you with its gaiety.

A guinea pig family lives very closely together. When they make expeditions, father and mother take the children between them so that no one gets lost.

Breeds and Colors

The House Pet of the Indians

The native habitat of the guinea pig is Central and South America. There the wild cavy is distributed throughout the entire continent. Geological evidence suggests that guinea pigs have been around for 35 to 40 million years. Several years ago excavations in central Peru, in settlements at altitudes of some 13,000 feet (4000 m), indicated that guinea pigs were domesticated long before Columbus discovered America. There archaeologists found guinea pig skulls, and by the changes in them they could establish that domestication took place between 9000 and 3000 B.C. Clearly the animals sought the protection and warmth of human habitations and nourished themselves with kitchen waste. At first they were tolerated by humans, then bred and used. For the Incas they were not only a source of meat but also served as sacrificial animals for the sun god. Brown or white spotted animals were especially prized.

How the Guinea Pig Came to Europe

The Swiss zoologist Konrad Gesner reported as early as 1554 "about the Indian rabbit or piglet." In 1670 Dutch merchants who discovered the tame little animals in the Guyanas, at that time a Dutch colony, brought them home as pets for their children. The guinea pig adapted very quickly to its new environment and reproduced so quickly that animals bred in Holland were sold in France and England by 1680. At that time they were so expensive that only rich people could afford them. But that changed quickly, since guinea pigs are so easy to keep, feed, and breed. Although documentation is lacking, it seems safe to assume that immigrants from England and the Netherlands brought guinea pigs to America early in the eighteenth century.

Development of the Breeds

When and how the breeds and colors of guinea pigs developed is uncertain. Most likely they developed as with other domestic animals: through genetic changes (mutations) in color and coat length. Selective breeding by humans helped to create the breeds and colors that we know today.

In England and Holland specific breeds are bred to an established standard, and prizes for the best animals are awarded at yearly shows. To date, standards for guinea pigs have not been established in the United States or Canada.

The various guinea pig breeds differ mainly in the appearance of their coats. There are smooth- or short-haired, Abyssinian, and long-haired guinea pigs, which occur in two varieties: the Peruvian and the sheltie.

There are also two categories that define the color or markings of guinea pigs: they are referred to as *self* or *marked*. Self guinea pigs possess a single, consistent fur coloring. Marked guinea pigs are patterned and have two or more colors.

Guinea pigs are rodents and tackle everything in the house that appears to be gnawable, even electric wires, which, unfortunately, often leads to fatal accidents. Watch your animal when you have it out for exercise. This is the only way you can prevent damage or accidents.

Something smells here.

Eye to eye with a rival.

Short-Haired Breeds

The English guinea pig has short hair, lying close to the body, and has been bred in the following colors:

• Agouti: These most resemble their wild ancestors in color. The gray shimmer of the fur, which comes from the various color zones of every single hair, is important. The base of the hair is silvery white, then becomes reddish to yellowish brown, while the hair tip is almost black. Stripes, spots, and brindling are not permitted in this breed. There are the colors gold, gray, silver, and cinnabar—all with dark eyes— and salmon, with red eyes.

• Brindle: Regular distribution of small flecks in red and black, with dark eyes.

• Monochrome: These guinea pigs are known to be especially sturdy and hardy. The colors should be the same over the whole body. There are white, cream, ochre, red, chocolate, and black—all with dark eyes—and white, lilac, beige, and gold—with red eyes. Pure white guinea pigs with red eyes are called albinos. They have dark spots on the nose, ears, and feet— so-called cold spots, since they are most noticeable in cold conditions.

• Himalaya: White with a dark mask; dark ears and feet; dark eyes.

• Dutch: The same color on both sides of the head (white blaze between) and rear third of the body (in the colors black, chocolate, red or agouti), the rest white; dark eyes.

Peaceful separation.

In the photos:
*Dominance rank-
ing. There's no
place in a guinea
pig group for two
boars. Only the
male that has
proved himself
strongest in a battle
for dominance has
the say in the herd.*

• Japanese: One side of the head
red, the other side black, alternating
both colors on both sides of the body,
as evenly divided as possible; dark
eyes.
• Russian: White with dark mask;
dark ears and feet; red eyes. In black
and chocolate.
• Tortoiseshell: As even a distribution
as possible of same-size spots in red
and black (diamond design); dark eyes.
• Tortoiseshell and white (tricolor): As
even as possible a distribution of
same-size spots of color. On each
body side three colors (black, red,
white); dark eyes.
  The last two color lines are com-
monly known as English spotted
guinea pigs.

Guinea Pigs with Special Hair Structure

• English crested guinea pig: Like a
monochrome English guinea pig but
with a single same-color whorl on its
forehead.
• American crested guinea pig: Like a
monochrome English guinea pig, but
with a single whorl of a different color
on the forehead.
• Abyssinian guinea pig: Known as
the rosette guinea pig, with hair growing in whorls that are evenly distributed
all over its body. Colors can be black,
white, red, tricolor, tortoiseshell, motley,
agouti, brindle, and frosted (red and black).
• Satin guinea pig: Short, smooth, but
very shiny fur. In the colors cream,
gold, and red.

• Rex guinea pig: Hair texture like that of a rex cat (curly or wavy plush-like fur).

Long-Haired Breeds

These are characterized by a silky fur that can grow 6 to 8 inches (15 to 20 cm) long. They are also known as angora guinea pigs. They are bred in many colors and color combinations, of which the rarest are the single-colored ones.

• Sheltie: Long, silky, thick hair without whorls; short hair on the head.
• Peruvian guinea pig: Long, thick, and shining fur with whorls distributed all over the body.

Differences Between Wild and Tame Guinea Pigs

	Wild	Tame
Body Build	Small, with long back legs	Roundish, plumper all over
Head	Pointed nose	Blunt
Coat	Short-haired, rough, gray-brown shot through with black (wild animal color)	Short-haired, smooth or with whorls, long-haired, many colors
Eye color	Dark	Dark and red
Inner organs	Small stomach, short small intestine, long cecum and large intestine	Large stomach, long small intestine, short cecum and large intestine
Feces	Abundant	Little
Special characteristics	Can leap as high as 29½ inches (¾ m).	

Learning to Understand Guinea Pigs

Zoological Classification

The guinea pig has nothing in common with the pig. Rather, it belongs to the large order of rodents, all of which have a jaw with rootless, constantly growing incisors and a large gap (diastema) between the incisors and the molars. Within the zoological classification system, which is divided into a multitude of super- and subfamilies, we are primarily interested in the genus *Cavia,* for here we find the primitive form of the tame guinea pig, the Tschudi guinea pig native to central Chile (named for the Swiss–South American explorer J.J. von Tschudi). Around the middle of the 19th century, when he was traveling in Peru, Tschudi encountered guinea pigs in the Indian huts that "ran across the faces and bodies of the sleepers all night long."

Guinea Pig Ancestors

The Tschudi guinea pigs appear at altitudes of up to 13,780 feet (4200 m). Small groups of five to ten animals live together in burrows, which they either dig themselves or take over from other animals. Only at night do they dare to creep out of their hiding places and run along firmly trampled paths through the dense grass to their feeding places. They differ substantially from domestic guinea pigs in appearance and internally (see table, page 50). They are plant eaters. From time to time, the whole year through, they bring from one to four young into the world. These are precocial, are nursed by the mother for three weeks, and are sexually mature at eight to ten weeks.

Wild Relatives

The wild relatives of the domestic guinea pig are abundant and varied. From the appearance and behavior of some of them, one would hardly believe that they are related. I'd like to introduce a few here:

Capybara: It grows to be 4 feet (1.3 m) long, weighs 110 pounds (50 kg), and is the largest living rodent. The capybara, which in Indian means "lord of the grasses," lives in woods with dense undergrowth in the vicinity of water and is an outstanding swimmer and diver.

Mara: Wrongly also called pampas hare, because it looks like a hare, it can be up to 29 inches (75 cm) long and weigh 20 to 35 pounds (9 to 16 kg). It can run very fast, jump as far as 2 yards (2 m), and dig deep, broad burrows. Its habitats are dry savannas and thickets.

Rock cavy: It is also called Moko and is about as large as the guinea pig. It lives under boulders and in burrows, can spring from rock to rock with a sleepwalker's confidence, and climb up trees to eat leaves. It can even climb smooth cement and glass brick walls, as was reported by the Berlin zoo director Ludwig Heck.

False paca or long-tailed paca: This rare, third largest rodent in the

Out in the wild the guinea pig must hone all its capabilities daily to survive the great number of its enemies. It has to find a safe burrow and succeed in its search for food.

All eyes, nose, and ears, the guinea pig explores its surroundings.

world is probably threatened with extinction. It can sit upright on its hind legs, has a rough coat, a large mustache, and quite a long tail.

Nutria: This animal is also known as a coypu. It digs its burrow in the sloping banks of streams and lakes and likes to stay in the water. Its skin is greatly prized as a fur.

Guinea Pig Names

In the German-speaking countries the name *Meerschweinchen,* "sea piglet," describes a small animal that came from across the sea and that looks and squeals like a little pig.

In Holland it is called *Guinees biggetje* or *Cavia.* The former means "guinea pig," or a piglet that was sold for one guinea, an old English gold coin. *Cavia,* the common designation today, is the Latin genus name.

In France the guinea pig is called *cochon d'Inde,* which means "pig from the Indies."

The Spaniards gave it the name *conejillo de Indias,* that is, "the little rabbit from the Indies," the closest to its zoological classification as a rodent.

The Domestic Guinea Pig
(Cavia aperea porcellus)

Order: Rodentia.
Suborder: Caviomorpha.
Family: Caviidae.
Genus: *Cavia.*
Size: 8 to 13½ inches (20 to 35 cm).
Weight: Male up to 63 ounces (1800 g); female up to 38½ ounces (1100 g).
Life-style: Herd animal.
Life expectancy: 5 to 10 years.
Distribution: South and Central America.
Domestication: Between 9000 and 3000 B.C.

Communal Life in the Herd

I have often mentioned that guinea pigs are very peaceful and sociable animals. It is part of their survival strategy to draw together in a herd, not to try to get each other's food, scarcely ever to tussle or fight. In so doing, they observe very strict dominance ranking. There is no place for two boars in any guinea pig family. Only the one who has shown himself the strongest in the battle for dominance may lead his harem. All other males are forbidden to mate with any females. So long as they are young, the males form their own groups at the edges of a family. When they are mature, they pick out a female and establish a new family.

The battle for dominance: At first the males try to threaten each other. They stiffen their legs so as to appear larger, let out a hissing rattle, chatter their teeth, and circle each other slowly. Thus each will get access to the side of the other to be able to administer a bite. Finally, they spring at each other and bite in the neck or the chest. This can last up to five minutes and is repeated until one male finally submits. The weaker is now driven from the herd.

In the cage it will eke out an unhappy existence from now on. It will be driven mercilessly from the feeding place, will find no place to sleep, and will starve to death if no one understands and removes it.

The lead female strives for rank among her contemporaries and younger animals. In doing so she often exhibits special behavior. Sitting on her hind legs, she twists her rear end slowly back and forth and chatters her teeth. Often the lead boar must interfere, as when the lead female and a female of lower rank do not get along.

Dealing with the young: As long

Before the altercation with a rival, the male makes himself "big" by stiffening his legs and raising himself up. Often the matter is ended with this impressing behavior alone.

network of tramped-down pathways between their burrows and feeding places. Here they know their way around very well and can flee rapidly. They move swiftly and agilely through the highest grass so as not to be easily discovered by their enemies. They always keep contact with one another; that is, they trip behind one another like a line of geese and lead the young between them. They communicate with gurgling sounds, which are never completely silenced. When they graze one of the animals sits to one side and keeps watch. At the smallest sound or change in the surroundings, the animal squeals, whereupon they all rush for safety. When a guinea pig has no alternative, it will play dead, which will sometimes deceive its enemy. Nature has also provided a "trick," so to speak, to keep the guinea pig from extinction: rapid reproduction.

as they are quite small, the young form small grazing groups with the females. They are nursed not only by their own mothers but also by other milk-producing females. When one of them feels abandoned, it squeals long and loudly until its mother hears. She approaches cooing, makes nose contact, licks its face, and leads it back to the group. From two weeks on the young also begin to follow the lead male, which weans them from the mother. They stop nursing after three weeks.

Behavior in the cage: Since in the cage there are no opportunities for escape, you must take care to remove the young males at the latest with the attainment of sexual maturity, at nine to ten weeks. This is necessary not only to avoid fights but also to prevent too much uncontrolled breeding.

Survival Strategy

Guinea pigs are by nature defenseless animals. But they possess capabilities that allow them to survive despite a large number of enemies, such as snakes, foxes, or birds of prey. They lay down a many-branched

How Guinea Pigs Communicate

Anyone who wants to understand the language of guinea pigs must listen as well as watch carefully, for the sounds that guinea pigs make are often with associated a particular body language. Almost everyone knows the long, demanding squeal of a guinea pig. It sounds like the whistle of a tea kettle, is an unmistakable begging for food, and is the only sound that the guinea pig uses exclusively for humans.

The peeping or complaining squeaking that a baby utters if it has gotten lost, its mother or siblings are not immediately visible, or some other sound makes it anxious, is the first sound the guinea pig masters. Even when kept singly the animals peep and thus ask for contact. Just as the mother runs up cooing reassuringly and, through gentle gurgling, signals protection and warmth, we should reassure our little charge.

Gurgling is a sound that expresses general contentment. If, in addition, the guinea pig leaps, it is a sign that it is in good spirit. A growling grunt to another animal is the friendliest kind of greeting. Family members grunt this way to one another if they meet outside. They sniff each other's noses while doing so. A weaker animal greets a stronger one with a rumbling, sinking its head as it does so—also to humans—and thus asks for a truce. If the gesture is not understood, the anxiety rumble turns to an angry chattering of teeth, which is the only threat the guinea pigs know. This teeth clacking is the forerunner of a battle for dominance, and usually it stops there. Therefore, leave your animal alone when it chatters threateningly; otherwise a strong bite can follow.

Finally, the rumbling rattle that the

When guinea pigs explore their surroundings, they start out on the same paths in all directions over and over again. Since they are defenseless animals and must protect themselves from many enemies, they lay down this network of beaten pathways to be able to whisk agilely and deviously to their lairs.

Body Language

What the Guinea Pig Does	What It Means
Touches other's nose	Sniffing contact
Rises up with knees stiffened	Threat posture
Lifts the head at right angles	Sign of strength
Shows teeth with mouth wide open	Female warning off a too importunate male
Stretches	Comfort, relaxation
Leaps	High spirits, good mood
Lies motionless on back	Defense, playing dead
Stands on hind legs	Reaching for food
Stretches head forward	Watchfulness
Draws in legs, presses against the wall	Helplessness, need for protection

A flowerpot makes a very good hideaway.

male makes when he comes near a female in heat accompanies mating. Guinea pigs are also supposed to utter a singing or songlike squeal. This was discovered by a Finnish zoologist. At the sound of the song, he reported, all the members of the family were silent for a moment and listened alertly. The meaning of the song is not yet known.

How Guinea Pigs Hear, See, and Smell

Guinea pigs **hear** extremely well. They can perceive high sounds in a range of up to 30 kHz, whereas humans can only hear sounds up to 20 kHz. The fact that they have developed such a varied "vocabulary" shows how much guinea pigs depend on their hearing. They react much more intensely to aural stimuli than to visual ones. For example, the guinea pig mother does not move if she sees her little one endangered, but she comes immediately if she hears it squeal. Guinea pigs quickly learn to respond to a particular sound. They recognize the step of their human partner from quite a distance away and react to particular noises that have to do with feeding. My guinea pigs begin a spirited concert of squeals at the clatter of the bowl in which I gather the greens. I knew of other guinea pigs that began to squeal when the door of the vegetable bin was opened and their food taken out.

Guinea pigs also **see** very well. Their angle of vision is quite large, so that they can perceive enemies from the front, the sides, or from above. Experiments have shown that guinea pigs can distinguish colors very well,

There's room for more in the box. The third is already on the way.

especially yellow, red, and blue, but also orange, violet, and green.

Guinea pigs don't **smell** as well as dogs, but considerably better than humans. An animal from another group is perceived by smell, and various members of the human family will be differentiated by their smell. My guinea pigs reacted particularly negatively to my cousin, who lived for a while in our large family. For the longest time we couldn't explain it, until she happened to change her perfume. Then we realized that the animals could not smell the old perfume and thus literally could not smell my cousin.

What Guinea Pigs Can Learn

Guinea pigs are by no means the boring animals they are sometimes supposed to be. Everything that I have imparted so far shows that they are lovable, lively creatures, with capabilities for being trained. You will be astonished at how quickly your guinea pig will learn once you begin to engage its intelligence. Naturally, some training is necessary, but consider that what keeps the guinea pig going in the wild is not called upon in its life as a pet. I have already spoken of the guinea pig's ability to distinguish color. You can try the following experiment with your pet: Place same-shaped bowls in different colors at some distance from one another (about 23 inches [60 cm])—for example a red, a yellow, a green, and a blue bowl. Only the red is filled with corn feed; the others are left empty. You should fill it with feed just before you begin the experiment, so that the animal won't be led to the right spot by the smell. Now let the guinea pig, which should be

In the photos: *A hideaway is a necessity of life. In the wild, guinea pigs, which are defenseless animals, can save themselves from their enemies only by lightning swift flight to their burrows.*

"Spoken Language"

What the Guinea Pig Utters	What It Means
Murmurs, gurgles, grunts	Contentment, comfort, shared feeling (contact through sound)
Squeals, squeaks	Warning, young's cry of loneliness, fear, pain, begging for food (reserved for humans)
Cooing	Reassurance
Rattles, hisses, teeth clacking	Aggression, threatening, warning opponent
Growls, grunts, rattling	Male arousal sounds

hungry, run from the other end of the room to the bowls. When it has found the filled bowl, take it away at once and let the animal look again. At some point your pet will understand what is going on and will always go to the red bowl, even if you change the order in which the bowls are placed. That it then may be difficult to change it was reported to me by a friend who used a

Something isn't right. Alertly the guinea pig extends its head and tries with all its senses to determine if danger threatens.

red bowl to train her guinea pig. When for some reason this bowl had to be discarded and she could only get a blue bowl, Buttons kept hesitating to eat out of it.

Guinea pigs also respond to music. A friend of my children always played his flute when he gave his pet its food. And it was very amusing to watch how eagerly that guinea pig ran up every time the flute was played.

As has been observed, it's in connection with food that the guinea pig's zeal for learning is greatest. This should not induce you to be too generous with treats, even if you are touched at how hard the animal works for them. The mother of a friend reported to me that her guinea pig always squealed whenever she passed the cage and it was hungry. She was the one who fed it. Otherwise it squeaked—but entirely differently—when it heard my friend's step on the stairs. In this way the mother knew exactly whether it was her daughter who was coming home.

Index

Color photos are indicated in **boldface** type.

Expertly Written Manuals For Premium Pet Care!

"Clear, concise … written in simple, nontechnical language." –Booklist

Hamsters
A Complete Pet Owner's Manual
—Plus More Than 40 Full-Color Photos

Cats
A Complete Pet Owner's Manual
With a Special Chapter: Understanding Cats

Rabbits
A Complete Pet Owner's Manual
With a Special Chapter: Understanding Rabbits —Plus More Than 40 Full-Color Photos

Guinea Pigs
A Complete Pet Owner's Manual
Special Chapter: Understanding Guinea Pigs Full-Color Photos

PET OWNER'S MANUALS

African Gray Parrots (3773-1)
Amazon Parrots (4035-X)
Bantams (3687-5)
Beagles (3829-0)
Beekeeping (4089-9)
Boxers (4036-8)
Canaries (4611-0)
Cats (4442-8)
Chinchillas (4037-6)
Chow-Chows (3952-1)
Cichlids (4597-1)
Cockatiels (4610-2)
Cockatoos (4159-3)
Dachshunds (2888-0)
Doberman Pinschers (2999-2)
Dwarf Rabbits (3669-7)
Feeding and Sheltering
   Backyard Birds (4252-2)
Feeding and Sheltering
   European Birds (2858-9)
Ferrets (2976-3)
Gerbils (3725-1)
The German Shepherd Dog (2982-8)
Golden Retrievers (3793-6)
Goldfish (2975-5)
Gouldian Finches (4523-8)
Guinea Pigs (4612-9)
Hamsters (4439-8)
Killifish (4475-4)
Labrador Retrievers (3792-8)
Lhasa Apsos (3950-5)
Lizards in the Terrarium (3925-4)
Longhaired Cats (2803-1)
Lovebirds (3726-X)
Mice (2921-6)
Mutts (4126-7)
Mynahs (3688-3)
Parakeets (4437-1)
Parrots (2630-6)
Persian Cats (4405-3)
Pigeons (4044-9)
Ponies (2856-2)
Poodles (2812-0)
Rabbits (4440-1)
Rottweilers (4483-5)
Schnauzers (3949-1)
Sheep (4091-0)
Shetland Sheepdogs (4264-6)
Shih Tzus (4524-6)
Siberian Huskies (4265-4)
Snakes (2813-9)
Spaniels (2424-9)
Tropical Fish (2686-1)
Turtles (2631-4)
Yorkshire Terriers (4406-1)
Zebra Finches (3497-X)

Paperback, 64–80 pp., 6½" x 7⅞",
over 50 illustrations including more
than 20 full-color photos in each
ISBN PREFIX: 0–8120

BARRON'S

Perfect for Pet Owners!

PET OWNER'S MANUALS

Over 50 illustrations per book (20 or more color photos), 72–80 pp., paperback.

AFRICAN GRAY PARROTS (3773-1)
AMAZON PARROTS (4035-X)
BANTAMS (3687-5)
BEAGLES (3829-0)
BEEKEEPING (4089-9)
BOSTON TERRIERS (1696-3)
BOXERS (4036-8)
CANARIES (4611-0)
CATS (4442-8)
CHINCHILLAS (4037-6)
CHOW-CHOWS (3952-1)
CICHLIDS (4597-1)
COCKATIELS (4610-2)
COCKATOOS (4159-3)
CONURES (4880-6)
DACHSHUNDS (1843-5)
DALMATIANS (4605-6)
DISCUS FISH (4669-2)
DOBERMAN PINSCHERS (2999-2)
DOGS (4822-9)
DWARF RABBITS (1352-2)
ENGLISH SPRINGER SPANIELS (1778-1)
FEEDING AND SHELTERING BACKYARD
    BIRDS (4252-2)
FEEDING AND SHELTERING EUROPEAN
    BIRDS (2858-9)
FERRETS (2976-3)
GERBILS (3725-1)
GERMAN SHEPHERDS (2982-8)
GOLDEN RETRIEVERS (3793-6)
GOLDFISH (2975-5)
GOULDIAN FINCHES (4523-8)
GUINEA PIGS (4612-9)
HAMSTERS (4439-8)
IRISH SETTERS (4663-3)
KEESHONDEN (1560-6)
KILLIFISH (4475-4)
LABRADOR RETRIEVERS (3792-8)
LHASA APSOS (3950-5)
LIZARDS IN THE TERRARIUM (3925-4)
LONGHAIRED CATS (2803-1)
LONG-TAILED PARAKEETS (1351-4)
LORIES AND LORIKEETS (1567-3)
LOVEBIRDS (3726-X)

MACAWS (4768-0)
MICE (2921-6)
MINIATURE PIGS (1356-5)
MUTTS (4126-7)
MYNAHS (3688-3)
PARAKEETS (4437-1)
PARROTS (4823-7)
PERSIAN CATS (4405-3)
PIGEONS (4044-9)
POMERANIANS (4670-6)
PONIES (2856-2)
POODLES (2812-0)
RABBITS (4440-1)
RATS (4535-1)
ROTTWEILERS (4483-5)
SCHNAUZERS (3949-1)
SHAR-PEI (4334-2)
SHEEP (4091-0)
SHETLAND SHEEPDOGS (4264-6)
SHIH TZUS (4524-6)
SIAMESE CATS (4764-8)
SIBERIAN HUSKIES (4265-4)
SNAKES (2813-9)
SPANIELS (2424-9)
TROPICAL FISH (4700-1)
TURTLES (4702-8)
YORKSHIRE TERRIERS (4406-1)
ZEBRA FINCHES (3497-X)

NEW PET HANDBOOKS

Detailed, illustrated profiles (40–60 color photos), 144 pp., paperback.

NEW AQUARIUM FISH HANDBOOK
    (3682-4)
NEW AUSTRALIAN PARAKEET
    HANDBOOK (4739-7)
NEW BIRD HANDBOOK (4157-7)
NEW CANARY HANDBOOK (4879-2)
NEW CAT HANDBOOK (2922-4)
NEW COCKATIEL HANDBOOK (4201-8)
NEW DOG HANDBOOK (2857-0)
NEW DUCK HANDBOOK (4088-0)
NEW FINCH HANDBOOK (2859-7)
NEW GOAT HANDBOOK (4090-2)
NEW PARAKEET HANDBOOK (2985-2)
NEW PARROT HANDBOOK (3729-4)
NEW RABBIT HANDBOOK (4202-6)

NEW SALTWATER AQUARIUM
    HANDBOOK (4482-7)
NEW SOFTBILL HANDBOOK (4075-9)
NEW TERRIER HANDBOOK (3951-3)

REFERENCE BOOKS

Comprehensive, lavishly illustrated references (60–300 color photos), 136–176 pp., hardcover & paperback.

AQUARIUM FISH (1350-6)
AQUARIUM FISH BREEDING (4474-6)
AQUARIUM FISH SURVIVAL MANUAL
    (5686-8)
AQUARIUM PLANTS MANUAL (1687-4)
BEFORE YOU BUY THAT PUPPY (1750-1)
BEST PET NAME BOOK EVER, THE
    (4258-1)
CARING FOR YOUR SICK CAT (1726-9)
CAT CARE MANUAL (5765-1)
CIVILIZING YOUR PUPPY (4953-5)
COMMUNICATING WITH YOUR DOG
    (4203-4)
COMPLETE BOOK OF BUDGERIGARS
    (6059-8)
COMPLETE BOOK OF CAT CARE (4613-7)
COMPLETE BOOK OF DOG CARE (4158-5)
COMPLETE BOOK OF PARROTS (5971-9)
DOG CARE MANUAL (5764-3)
FEEDING YOUR PET BIRD (1521-3)
GOLDFISH AND ORNAMENTAL CARP
    (5634-5)
GUIDE TO A WELL BEHAVED CAT
    (1476-6)
GUIDE TO HOME PET GROOMING
    (4298-0)
HEALTHY DOG, HAPPY DOG (1842-7)
HOP TO IT: A Guide to Training Your Pet
    Rabbit (4551-3)
HORSE CARE MANUAL (5795-3)
HOW TO TALK TO YOUR CAT (1749-8)
HOW TO TEACH YOUR OLD DOG
    NEW TRICKS (4544-0)
LABYRINTH FISH (5635-3)
MACAWS (6073-3)
NONVENOMOUS SNAKES (5632-9)
WATER PLANTS IN THE AQUARIUM
    (3926-2)

Barron's Educational Series, Inc. • 250 Wireless Blvd., Hauppauge, NY 11788
Call toll-free: 1-800-645-3476 • In Canada: Georgetown Book Warehouse
34 Armstrong Ave., Georgetown, Ont. L7G 4R9 • Call toll-free: 1-800-247-7160
ISBN prefix: 0-8120 • Order from your favorite book or pet store

Important Note

Some sicknesses are contagious to humans (see page 35). If your guinea pig shows any signs of infection (see page 39), you should not fail to get the advice of a veterinarian and if you have any doubts at all, go to a doctor yourself. There are people who are allergic to animal hair. If you are not sure, check with your doctor before you get a guinea pig.

English translation © Copyright 1991
by Barron's Educational Series, Inc.

© Copyright 1990 by Gräfe and Unzer
GmbH, Munich, West Germany
The title of the German book is
Meerschweinen

Translated from the German by Elizabeth
D. Crawford

All rights reserved.
No part of this book may be reproduced in
any form, by photostat, microfilm, xerogra-
phy, or any other means, or incorporated
into any information retrieval system, elec-
tronic or mechanical, without the written
permission of the copyright owner.

All inquiries should be addressed to:
Barron's Educational Series, Inc.
250 Wireless Boulevard
Hauppauge, NY 11788

Library of Congress Catalog Card Number
90–26577

International Standard Book Number
0-8120-4612-9

**Library of Congress Cataloging-in-Publication
Data**

Behrend, Katrin.
[Meerschweinen. English]
Guinea pigs : proper care and understanding :
expert advice for appropriate maintenance /
Katrin Behrend ; translated from the German by
Elizabeth D.Crawford ; color photographs, Karin
Skogstad ; drawings by György Jankovics ;
consulting editor, Lucia Vriends-Parent.
  p.   cm.
Translation of: Meerschweinen.
Includes index.
ISBN 0-8120-4612-9
1. Guinea pigs as pets.   I. Title.
SF459.G9B4413   1991
636'.93234–dc20   90-26577
                                CIP

Printed in Hong Kong

4   4900   9